VOICE OF A SOUL

AN EMOTIONAL FLOW

MRS. U. MARAGATHAM

DEDICATION

In the memory of my soulMr. K. MOHAN, (C.I., TNEB)

This book is solely dedicated

- To my soul, the one who stands behind all my success.

Contents

Contents

Contents

Contents

Contents

Disclaimer

This cute compilation of 100 poems is a plagiarism free content of write ups on various topics.

The author guarantees the originality of her own write ups.

Preface

"POETRY IS WHEN AN EMOTION HAS ITS THOUGHT AND THE THOUGHT HAS FOUND WORDS." - Robert Frost

Poetry is the spontaneous overflow of powerful feelings. It takes its origin from the emotions recollected in tranquility as William Wordsworth said.

A poet is a person who is passionately in love with the language. The author of the book as a language lover started her writing during the pandemic. She discovered herself as a writer by joining the CREATIVE WRITERS GROUP, a group of many eminent writers cum teachers. Day by day, she could see the immense change in her style of writing. As a result here comes the "VOICE OF A SOUL", an ornament with hundred beads to adore the beauty of verses. With the help of some well- wishers support and encouragement this budding poetess has created this marvellous piece of poetry. No doubt, this book will surely be a fabulous feast for language lovers and poetry lovers.

Editor's Note

Mrs. S. SUMATHI, M.A., B.Ed.,SRI KGS HSS,
ADUTHURAI,THANJAVUR DT.

My dear friend,

Your creativity never ends

With a majestic, matured mind

One of the best human to find.

My dear teacher,

Being a motivator

Always encourages the nation's pillars,

The future generations' finest tuner.

My dear poetess,

Always beget success

Keep on moving in the path of progress,

With your thoughts and verses to impress.

From The Pen Of The Editor

Mr. S. SANTHANAMBUSINESSMAN

Mrs. Maragatham, teacher
Known for her poem's nature
Innovative thoughts in word
Creative writings to world.
Written poems few hundred
All of them are so wondered
We can feel her happiness,
Sorrow, love and faithfulness.
Some of them are nature bound
And some have the social ground.
All her poems express us
Emotions and advices.

Verses in "Voice of a Soul"

On the whole she reached her goal

We all wish her to publish

More collections in English.

Acknowledgements

I owe the credit of this book "Voice of a soul" to Mrs. D. Brinda, Graduate Teacher

(English),GHS, Melapattampakkam, Cuddalore Dt. She has been motivating and encouraging a lot of teachers, students and other language lovers to write. I am one among them. A few words of gratitude for her tireless efforts is not enough. Hereby I submit my heartfelt thanks for her encouragement.

I express my sincere gratitude to our Rev. Correspondent Mr. K. Ramesh, Sri Saraswathi Patasala GHSS, most respected Headmistress Mrs. K. Thamil Selvi , lovable Assistant Headmistress Mrs. K. Latha and my dear colleagues.

I express my deepest gratitude to Mrs. D. Brinda, Graduate Teacher(English), GHS, Melpattampakkam and Mr. M. Chelliah, Senior Manager, Indian Bank, Kovai, also an ardent supporter of my poetic work, for contributing their fantastic foreword for this collection of poems. They are really boosters for me to climb my success ladder.

I sincerely record my thanks to Mrs. S.Sumathi M.A.B.Ed., Graduate Teacher (English), SRI KGS HSS, Aduthurai, who first voluntarily and readily gave her consent in editing my poems and guided me in each and every step of my publication. Under her guidance only this possibility came into existence. The great efforts and effective measures she took for my publication cannot be just expressed in words. I pray the Almighty for her successful career to reach the ultimate goal.

I also thank Mr. S.Santhanam, a business man from Tirunelveli and Mrs. R. Jael Beulah, GHSS, Mangalam, Thiruvannamalai district for spending their precious time in editing. Many of their ideas and suggestions, no doubt adds beauty to my poems.

My special thanks to Mrs. J. Ezhil, M.A.B.Ed., Graduate Teacher (English), Sri Saraswathi Patasala GHSS, Kumbakonam, one of my colleagues and best friend, also the introducer of me to the Creative Writers group. At the outset, I thank my sister and my dear sons for supporting me in all my aspects. I thank one and all who worked and supported for this wonderful collection of poems.

Foreword

Mr. M. CHELLIAH, Senior Manager, Indian Bank, Kovai

All good things starts with the mother, In the same way the set of poem starts with praising the Mother and it goes on praising the mother's nature, mother's dream, mother's love...

A mother of two sons Mrs. Maragatham has come out with sizzling hundred poems on dreams, desires, dejection, destiny, devotion, daddy and goes on and on.

The pen from Mrs. Maragatham has just started blooming word flowers as poetry ... it's just a beginning and already the scent of the flowers are spreading. I am sure a big garden of poetry awaits from her.

A best poetry starts from the love of nature.. no wonder Mrs. Maragatham, a lover of mother nature has penned down with wonderful set of poems.

I am sure it will be a treat for poet admirers.

I wish sucess in her endeavour as poet.

Expecting many such short poems in coming days...

It's just hundred...it will be thousand next and goes on

I wish her all the best ...let her pen flows with flower of words and words...

Mr. M. Chelliah..

Foreword

Mrs. D. BRINDA,Graduate Teacher (English),GHS,
Melpattampakkam,Cuddalore dt.

'Voice of a Soul' is a collection of 100 poems written by Mrs. U. Maragatham. In her first poem 'Son', she has expressed a lot about her son. All mothers learn so much from their kids, ups and downs, courage and strength, and last poem Namestry, is an acrostic poem for her own name Maragatham. Nature teaches a lot of lessons.All her poems are worth reading and very meaningful. Many of us are suffering from loneliness that is clearly depicted in her poem, 'I couldn't stay up all night.' When we read the poem like Painful heart, tears overflow, because they are so touching it brings the scene in front of our eyes. I believe she will soon compile an autobiography on her own. This book itself is like an autobiography. In most of the poems some sort of loneliness and isolation prevails in the author's mind. This is seen in many of her poems. For so many problems, there are no solution. A few poems have followed good rhyming words and rhyming scheme.She is one of the prominent and regular contributors of Creative writers WhatsApp group. She is very sincere, hard working and a good motivator of other writers. She encourages others by her reviews. She has written some different genre of poetry like Pyramid poem, an acrostic poem. They add spice to the book. Some poems are melancholic in nature but it is beautifully portrayed in a picturesque manner. A letter to the departed soul is really heart touching. She spends her time in depression. Her poems make the readers feel pity. It is more of personification. All her poems are well arranged and they evoke our feelings. There is healing mantras too in those poems. She has a lot of concern for mother earth, trees conservation, Environment, most of the titles itself elaborated what is inside the poem. Here and there the author adds spice to the readers. I love the poem 'The bond between you and me.' Her inner self is brought out very well. Caring for Differently abled is a fantastic poem and the lesson I learn from you gives a lot of lessons to learn. Hunger touches the heart and Dear soldiers is the real tribute to all the soldiers who safeguard our country from the problems in the borders. Hence, I conclude that this book will really be appreciated by all the readers. It will surely decorate the shelves of many libraries. I wish her all success.

Mrs. D. Brinda

1. WHEN I AM ABOUT TO WRITE

When I am about to write for the first time,
An instant sparkling in me is about my son
The one who gave me elixir in my life.
When he was an infant,
Leaning on my shoulder
He gave me enough courage and strengthened my mind.
When he started kneeling,
He taught me ups and downs in life.
When he started walking,
He forced me to go ahead.
When he started schooling,
He urged me to learn.
Now at the verge of his youthful,
He is supposed to be a friend of mine.
I am just a mother to my son
But he is not just a son to me
He is everything to me.

2. WHEN NATURE SPEAKS

When nature speaks to mankind
What will she say?
Will she blame for polluting her?
Will she forget to bestow her treasures?
Will she punish by upholding her primitive elements?
Will she deny her precious gifts?
She - the nature, the fruits and nuts on the growing trees,
The sunlight, the rain, the air, the beautiful landscapes,
The chirping voices of the enchanting birds,
What else to say?
Everything is still bestowed on us
Whatever we dump on her
She in turn nurtures us.
She- the nature is the existing and persisting god,
Praise and preach the Almighty.

3. I COULD STAY UP ALL NIGHT

I could stay up all night when
I have a deep thought on the happenings
Mostly undesirable, unforgettable issues.
I feel the loneliness on my part,
Pleading the whole night to take it apart.
To drive it away,
I got stuck into the cellular phone
Which would pluck my slumber
Making it still postpone,
Some of them could be spent with pleasure
As mind always goes in greed
For only pleasurable treasures.

4. PAINFUL HEART

• 4 •

I saw a lady on the roadside
Poverty ridden, mournful eyes, melancholic face,
Depressed mind, grief-stricken soul.
She stumbled as she rose
Looked in frustration the passersby.
Not many of them noticed her
Holding recklessly her torned filthy clothes
She made a painful move wandering like a nomad
I didn't know what she needed and the reason behind her state
When I neared, she stared at me and left
I was dumbfounded and stood still
I detected my heart aching as she departed
She left nothing but a painful heart in me.

5. BOOKS

Books are our treasures,
Books are our companions,
Books are our masters,
Books are our mentors,
Books are our admonitors.
The valuable treasures are in safety lockers,
The companions are beyond the bounds,
The masters are on the far sides,
The mentors are in ardent awaits,
The admonitors are in good expects.
The portable cellulars have taken the domicile
The periodic change of the globe would change things
One fine day books will take over the universe.

6. REMINISCENCE

Lots of reminiscences on queue,
What to share and what to leave,
However the instinct memories
Are those childhood days.
How can one ever forget all those plays
Streets were supposed to be the playing rooms,
Playmates of the nearby claimed to be the social website participants,
Leading powerful fellow of the group deemed to be the admin,
The proximate blogger constrained to be the forwarder,
Our playtime went hand in hand with all.
Gone are those days
No high tech can replace that relishing moments.
Yearning for those bygone days
Reminiscing a silhouette of the past thoughts..

7. WELCOME APRIL

•7•

We were told April means to open
What about nature.
The trees sprout the new leaves,
The flowers begin to bloom,
The weather forecasts it's cosiness,
The sky telecasts two zodiac signs,
The earth's atmosphere delivers meteor showers,
The Gregorian calendar celebrates it's fourth birth,
The smaller animals come out of their hibernation,
And needless to say,
The April month showers bring May flowers.

8. COMFORT ZONE

My comfort zone is my loneliness
At times I feel emptiness
Overwhelmed with bags of burdens,
Some sort of obstacles,
Stressed with handful of worries,
Unable to find solutions
I prefer myself postured in seclusion
Wiping out all undesirable confusion,
Discovering the clean slate of mind there upon,
Feeling safe and sound in my comfort zone.

9. NIGHTMARE

After a long tiresome effort,

I went to sleep to comfort.

Intermittently I had a slumber

Soon I realized someone

Holding me like a monster.

I managed to make a move

But felt as if in a groove,

I wished to raise my hands to gain

Which everything went out in vain.

I willed to utter chanting

To recover from the horrific happening.

My inner psyche judged it as an illusion

My intellect mind reasoned it as an scientific allusion

Eventually I came out from the terrible nightmare.

10. PYRAMID POETRY

Mother
Giver of Life
Always Caring
Unconditional Love
Wonderful personality
At times she might be rigid
Not at all showed her antipathy
Oftentimes she would be free and easy
To grasp her temperament is inexplicable
She handled everyone's conceptions exclusively
Oh! could have been the most blessed one on earth.

11. SOLITUDE

In the mechanised era,
Amongst the tight schedule
We plea for loneliness
At least for some hours,
To free ourselves from all hardships.
Solitude seems to be a gift in the middle ages
Nonetheless it happens to be a curse
In the declining years of life.
Automatically mind longs for own bonds
To pass through the elderliness.
Solitude is blissful for sometimes
Not all times.

12. TOMORROW

• 12 •

Tomorrow is the day
Waiting in a new way,
No matter something that delay,
Happens to be done the next day,
No need to take it as a stay,
It's a span of time to make the situation gay,
Don't let yourself in dismay.
Preparing the mind for tomorrow is a gateway
To move ourselves in our runway.

13. DEAR STUDENTS, THIS YEAR 2023,

A - Access your potentials

B - Benevolent to all

C - Care for others

D - Dedicate yourself in your duty

E - Enrich your skills F - Fulfil your wishes

G - Grasp the meaning of education H - Honour the elders

I - Ignore the invisible virus J - Justify your actions

K - Kind in your words L - Literate those who needs

M - Motivate yourself N - Neglect the backbiters

O - Obedient in all aspects P - Practice the best in you

Q - Qualify for competitions

R - Rectify the mistakes

S - Secure supreme success

T - Trigger your talents

U - Understand others feelings

V - Victory in reach

W - Work for the success

X - Xenial in nature

Y - Yearn for the pleasant life

Z - Zest the success of your career.

14. MY SUCCESS LADDER

I am happy about what I am now
But not satisfied in my whereabouts.
The success doesn't end here
By looking back and reminiscing the thoughts.
I could see many stairs of my successful ladder
My mother who inspired me a lot
Felt great and proud in me,
Taught to tackle tyring conditions.
My father who paved platform for my career,
My partner who let me to be self-determined,
My toddlers who made my life worthwhile,
Above all my comrades who stood together in all my hardships,
Who else to say?
Many stairs are still awaiting in my ladder
To witness my ultimate succession.

15. BEHIND THE MASK

Behind the mask lies today's fate
The unseen virus having it's parade,
In the beginnings adorned with proud,
As time goes by not of much regard.
Behind the mask, the sense organs felt uncomfort
Nevertheless that became to protect,
The face shield evaded the smiles
To retrieve everyone's lives.
Behind the mask of some uneasiness
Submissively lies our happiness.

16. WHEN I CLOSE MY EYES

When I close my eyes,
Lots of thoughts queue up
Reminisce about the happenings,
Some good, some bad.
Good ones go deep into the subconscious mind,
Bad ones begin to conquer us.
Mind and brain wrestle with each other
After a long struggle, mind forecasts.
The next day's routine work
The body beseeches to relax,
Accepting the request nap embraces
Alarming of the late night.

17. MISCHIEVOUS BABY

Oh baby! nay!
What have you done?
Whirling around yourself in the pile of fabrics
Organized strenuously in the rack,
Come out baby! Come with me!
I will take you to the kitchen.
Oh no! Don't shuffle the utensils
Then I have to carry out a lot
Come, my boy!
Let's have some pleasure
In the garden and cheer.
Oh stop! Don't pluck the flowers
Your tender hands will get hurt
Oh! Come on my little one!
I am totally wearied.
Running along with you the whole day
Enjoying every naughty doings of you
My mischievous boy!

18. MY INNER VOICE

My inner voice always alerts me
In a silent manner, I agree
I bound myself in challenging times
In rejoicement it induces to share happiness.
Sometimes my inner voice ventures me
To take apt decision in glee.
But in undesirable quandaries
It presses me to keep silence.
Whatever the case maybe
I always give ears to my inner voice.

19. IT'S NOT MY FAULT

It's not my fault
For I nurtured them with support,
Providing all the needs,
Beside with their views,
Planning for the future,
Indulge myself in pressure,
Still I could not satisfy
As they feel I pacify.
Is there any sign of partiality?
It's not my fault,
I am just a rationalist without any discrimination.
Soon the fact will reach them
I am waiting for that day.

20. DANCE - AN EXPRESSION WITHOUT A WORD

Dance is not only an art,
But also a skill to impart
Culture and tradition with heritage
Of course has many forms of age,
Replicates the hidden language of the soul,
Makes the performers do a rhythmic troll
May be solo or group staging
The physical exertion and emotional charming
Depicts the fascinating body language
Dance- an expression without words is a salvage.

21. POEM BY A TEACHER DURING LOCKDOWN PERIOD

My dearest wards,
More than three hundred and sixty five days gone
Without hearing the warm welcome
Good morning miss- a wonderful note by my children,
Casual enquiries of their turning up,
Every forty five minutes of the classroom,
Discussion of the lessons,
Interaction of the sessions,
Day-break enjoyments,
Small complaints of unimportant matters,
Satisfying them as mentors,
Evening sendoff with a hearty thank you,
We miss you all dear children,
Waiting for the day to come again
Are you all ok dear?

22. GREETINGS FROM A TEACHER AFTER THE LOCKDOWN

Welcome to school my dears,
Longing to see you after one and a half years,
Wishing to hear your welcome greetings,
Expecting your valuable presence for the coming days.
The first and foremost duty is
To prepare you for the school modus,
The motto is to inculcate basic manners.
The main role of imparting knowledge also matters
It's your presence my dear wards
That makes the classroom more essence.

23. LETTER TO THE DEPARTED - APPA

Dear Appa,

Why have you left this world?

You told mom that you would be with her,

How strong she felt in your shade,

Let the Almighty restore peace in heaven for you.

The charming face with ever smile

Majestic moustache, legendary walk,

When am I going to see you again?

I beseech you to give enough courage

To recover from the irretrievable loss.

I think God has given some assignment

To perform your duty in heaven's palace,

So you have left the earth earlier.

No worries Appa, I shall try to console your dear ones

But not sure whether they will.

24. LETTER TO THE DEPARTED - AMMA

Dear Amma,
Years had gone
You left me without a word
To perceive what had happened.
To my lovable mom,
Everything went out of my hand
Still now I am questioning myself
Is there anything wrong with me?
Did you try to say something?
The moment I saw the tears in your eyes at your last breath
I thought you had some trouble.
Later my inner sense understood
I beckon you ma please tell me
What did you wish to convey?

25. LETTER TO THE DEPARTED - BETTER HALF

Dear better half,

Days are going without you

Leaving us abandoned without a word.

Recalling your memories day by day

Things everything around us

Spot the presence (absence) of you

Oh God ! Give us the strength to push

The remaining days of our life.

I act as if I am recovering

But the departed soul could only know the truth behind.

Let me take this as the Creator's verdict

In turn, Oh Almighty! Restore him with peace in heaven.

26. QUESTION TO GOD

Who am I to ask?
Afterall I am just a creature of Him,
All the worldly beings created by Him,
He is the sole proprietor of all happenings.
I thank the Almighty if granted with happiness
While plunged in mournfulness, I just pray
Oh God! Gratify and help me to overthrow the miseries.
If at all I fortify myself to ask
Then I have only one question to ask
And one obligation to express
Why we people always yearn for the one we don't hold
Whatever bestowed on us is well and good
Bless a disease-free life for the leftover span.

27. GET WELL SOON

Get well soon
My mother land,
You have been disseminated
With the unseen virus.
We, the children of you
Day by day getting weaker,
Help us to gain good fortune
Save us from the deadly disease.
We promise you
We heed you
What you say by your gentle gesture
We have understood well
The responsibility of each and every individual
To get well soon.

28. THE WAY I TOOK WAS DIFFERENT

I wished to become a nurse

My mother wanted me to be an engineer

My father pointed me the role of a teacher

Others specified various fields

I heeded to my father's desire.

Now I am a teacher

Proudly and elegantly, I would say

This noble profession has shaped and moulded me,

Makes me to learn each day.

The way I took was not only different

But highly reputable and respectable.

29. BIRTHDAY WISHES TO MY SISTER

Happy birthday wishes

May God bless with all prosperities in life,

Your better half is one of the best gifts,

Your lovable children are the marvellous bumper prizes,

May the coming year brings success in your work,

All your hardships are going to yield sweet fruits.

I pray the Almighty to shower

Evergreen happiness on you

This is the one and only prayer for my well-wisher.

30. EDUCATION

Education - It's a single word
But has innumerable definitions,
Simply said gaining knowledge,
Acquisition of skill,
Process of being educated in educational institutions,
Preparing and qualifying the individuals to gain economy,
More and more views on education.
But the grassroot meaning of edu-care is:
Desirable Modification of behaviour
Yes and that means the real education.

31. HAPPY BIRTHDAY WISHES TO CW

I was in need of a platform to expose myself
By God's grace I got an entry to CW group,
With the help of my colleague cum friend.
At first I thought of writing some article
Mrs. Brinda Mam insisted me to write a poem
Aha! I can't write poems - I replied
You scribble dear - she motivated
Still now I am scribbling something
Members of CW encouraging with their reviews.
On this first birthday of our group
I would like to extend my wish
To publish a book of my own writings
An unquenchable thirst
Hope with all your encouragement and motivation
I can do it.
Happy birthday CW group.

32. THIS TOO SHALL PASS AWAY

What to say?

Is there a single problem?

Is there any solution?

If at all we overcome

The next step on with a different incarnation.

The day started with the unseen virus

That too counted on our record

To put an end to that monster

The whole world is waiting

Of course we are presented with handful of worries

We know how to handle

But we don't know how to fight

Against the deadly demon

However still we have the faith

That this too shall pass away.

33. LIFE IS LIKE A...

Life is like a clay
If moulded perfectly it gives gay
Else it happens to falsify
Yet it gives a chance to rectify.
Once our clay model is ready
Mind gets ready for glory
After all it's like a monkey
Jumping on things with flurry
Again the mind warns to dismantle
Now at least it helps to handle
Matters in a prominent style
Here comes the life's reconcile.

34. MY HEALING MANTRA IS

I shall overcome - this is my healing mantra
I shall overcome all the obstacles in my way
I shall overcome all the miseries blessed on me
I shall overcome all the difficulties in performing my tasks
I shall overcome all the challenges cast on me
I shall overcome all the negative impacts on me
With this special and powerful mantra
I shall walk through the rough road
Of my life with full breath.

35. POLLUTION FREE EARTH

Pollution free earth

Is it possible for the future birth?

Who is behind this hazardous scenario?

None other than the inhabitants.

The panchabhutas of our mother,

Five manifestations of our nature,

Lost their cleanliness and naturalness

To it's turn now it has taught us a lesson.

Past is past

Let's join hands to make a pollution free environment

Not just pondering only on this environment day alone

Go green and have an eco friendly biosphere.

36. I CAN'T LIVE WITHOUT YOU

Plants can't live without sunlight
Of course there are some exceptions
Life is also just like that.
I can live without a modular kitchen,
I can live without a sophisticated lifestyle,
I can live without ego,
But I can't live without the one
Who cares for me,
Who supports me in my hardships,
Who don't let my self-confidence level down.
They are none other than
My well-wishers, mentors and my dear friends.

37. EUPHORIC MOMENTS

At every stage of life,

There comes an euphoric moment.

During infantile, mother's warmth,

In childhood, father's unexpected presents,

Friends care on unhappy moments,

Teachers' encouragement in failure times,

The second I hold my degree crown,

The moment I stepped into my career,

The cherishable day when I'm bonded with my better half,

That wonderful day I gave birth to my children

And so my euphoric moments goes on.....

38. MY DAD - MY HERO

My dad - a hero to me

When I was young,

He had never spent much time with me

What ever thing I longed was not in a reach so easy.

After a hard struggle and on condition only I could succeed.

But the path I am traveling now was shown by him

On the other hand today what my children wish is

Very easily accessible for them

What's the difference?

I have patience towards my problems and their solutions

I feel my children missing out that,

That's what my hero had taught me and left..

39. STRANGE HABITS

I have some strange habits
Let me figure out with limits,
When indulged in grief
I would not like to lament even in brief,
Isolating myself trying to get over
Slowly prepares mind to recover,
Until such time my eyes fail to close
Getting better again I disclose
Having raw rice often,
Taking tea along with my tiffin
Also counts to my strange habits.

40. SALUTE TO DOCTORS

Doctors- the visible god,
Service minded, humanity natured,
Real warriors of the pandemic,
A tribute on this special day alone is
Just not enough for their contribution.
Restoring the lives of many
At the dead end is
Really a superior power.
On behalf of all our mankind
We salute our marvellous endeavour.

41. A PEACEFUL SLUMBER

A peaceful slumber
I wish to have sooner.
Lots and lots of deliberations,
Hurdles to conquer slumber
Mind struggles hard to win.
A slight nap starts with a lullaby
There arises so many queries
About the next day's plan.
Yes, at last slumber occupies
Out of weary mind and body.

42. THE BEST IN ME

• 42 •

The best in me
I can tolerate all my sufferings within me,
I expose my happiness to all,
But the miseries are suppressed
I express to my supporters rarely.
My patience towards anything
Of course I suggest the best in me
Even I don't have envy on anyone or anything
Cool! my best list persists.

43. GRIEF DISAPPEARS WHEN

Grief disappears when we stand
Against the cause of it,
To clear out all the hindrances,
Go deep routed into the grounds,
Erase the ill-feelings,
Figure out the remedies,
Switch over to the positive vibes,
Beyond everything have faith in the Almighty.
Happenings are the will of the Creator
Good or bad, accept life as such
There vanishes grief.

44. MY DEAR CHUMS

Chums, companions, comrades,
Soul mates, friends,
With so many names we have them.
Feeling safe and secure at times,
Bold and proud many a times,
A helping hand in need,
Soothing words in distress,
The most comfort zone of relaxation,
Above all a gentle word of gesture
"I am here for you.
Don't worry."
Who else - none other than our chums.

45. WHY ME?

Difficulties asked why me?
Life answers to overcome.
Sorrowfulness asked why me?
Life answers to tolerate.
Anger asked why me?
Life answers to pour out blusters.
Fear asked why me?
Life answers to avoid misdeeds.
All the negative aspects asked
why me?
Life answered to be positive.
Stay positive, stay blessed.

46. I MISS THESE THINGS THE MOST IN MY LIFE

I miss my parents the most in my life
When they were with me
I thought them as my solution.
When they left me I was abandoned
Slowly I gathered myself to face life
Many a things I sought was
Not within an easy reach.
I had to pass so many trials and errors
With all these so many missings
I understood -
Nothing can be achieved so easily
If achieved then it would be something.
That won't stay long with you.

47. THESE THINGS I LIKE IN MY FAVOURITE TEACHER

Reminiscing my thoughts backward
When I was in seventh standard,
I got attracted by my maths teacher
I could not point out why I liked her,
I liked the way she talked with us
I admired her teaching always,
Even I adorned her way of dressing
The hair style including.
I felt in grief when I missed
Her teaching in my eighth standard
Again in my tenth I was blessed,
With my favourite teacher
Whenever I hear the song
"Kannamma kannamma azhagu poonchilai"
My mind goes towards her.
Yes, my favourite teacher's name is
Kannamma.

48. INDEPENDENT - YET IN CHAINS

Independent India celebrates her 75th birthday
Stands with pride for unity in diversity.
The birth place of ancient religion is bound with leashes
Wealth of India attracted the British in early times.
The income inequality had paved a vast split - Survey reveals
When a girl walks safely in the midnight
Then only it's true independent- said Mahatma.
A big question arises in each one's mind
Have we achieved that independent defined?
It's not superfluous to negotiate-
Independent India- yet in chains.

49. IN THE END YOU HAVE ONLY YOURSELF

From womb to tomb
Life is not a blissful bloom.
Every step is a challenging one
Yet we expect a good fortune.
Blessed with our caretakers beside
Events are handled in abide.
The real checkmate comes in solo
At the end, there would be none to follow.

50. LIFE IS FULL OF CONTRADICTIONS

Life is a challenge - we know
If it's just an adventure, we can bow
Stress and agony, fear and pain,
Risks and hazards knock in vain,
Like thorns in the plant
Life is full of contradictions with grant,
Yet we all focus on the blossom
Thus goes our successful rhythm.

51. I'M SCARED OF...

I am not scared of any failure
Till my better half's departure.
The moment he left me abandoned
All my chores have got stunned,
Now I am scared of each and everything
The society that I am going to face,
The monstrous tasks in race,
The future of my children,
The restless remaining days with grief stricken.
Oh god! Give me back my life
Free me from my panic.

52. OBSTACLES CAN NEVER STOP YOU DEAR...

Obstacles follow us right from the birth

Even birth of an individual happens after so many obstacles.

Yes, obstacles can never stop me.

I crossed many hurdles in life

Will power, self confidence, faith in God,

Paved me to overcome and pushed to progress.

Problems approached with hidden solutions

Every trivial situation taught a lot

Hindrances moulded and remoulded to support further

What else - still preparing

The mind to face the impediments with patience.

53. WELCOME OCTOBER

Welcoming October triggers scintillating thoughts
The feminine powers-
Goddess Durga, Saraswathi and Lakshmi
Shower their divine supreme blessings,
Navarathri festival full of excitement and colours.
Also imparts the worship of tools and instruments.
Vijayadhasami celebrates the victory of good over evil
They are the providers of good fortune.

54. LIBERTY

Liberty is not just a word
It's a measure of unrestricted freedom to forward.
There is a saying - too much of anything
Is good for nothing
The unrestricted must be followed with a restriction
Then comes a clean slate of mind without fiction.
Liberty is enjoyable only
When it is understood fairly.

55. GOLDEN DAYS OF MY LIFE

Those days when I cared about nothing
Other than my playmates and plaything,
Glimpsing the scene of soorasamharam displayed on the shore,
Sitting on my father's shoulder,
Spectacular demonstration of delicious cuisines,
In neighbourhood's Patio on kaanum pongal with cohorts,
Eagerly waiting for the parcel 'rasa vadai' on Sunday mornings,
Day and night dreaming of the new dresses during festivals,
Spending hours and hours with mates on river beds,
Talking of simple things in enormous,
All those golden days had gone along with my early days
The only thing left is the remnants of the memories.

56. LET'S LIGHT THE WORLD

Let's light the world
With purity and piousness,
We have the future pillars in hand.
Let us teach them good virtues
To make the world violence- free,
Handle the genders with tenderness
Train them to fight against the iniquity,
Now you can see the world grow brighter.

57. PLEASURE IN SELF SACRIFICE

Sacrifice of delicious food during pregnancy,

Sacrifice of eatables at the time of lactation,

Sacrifice of leisure with playful kids,

Sacrifice of pain in work pressure,

Sacrifice of small enjoyments of family time,

Sacrifice of little expectations from dependents,

In all and above these self sacrifices lies the pleasure of a woman.

58. ANADIPLOSIS IN POETRY

Knowledge is Power,

Power is the authority,

Authority is a kind of specified liberty,

Liberty leads to attain potential,

Potential pave way to possibilities,

Possibilities help to achieve success,

Success makes our life divine.

59. FESTIVALS HELP CULTURAL DEVELOPMENTS

Festivals deliver happiness and enjoyments,
In that happiness lies the bonding.
Every festival has its unique peculiarity,
Promotes diversified glorious heritage,
Dignifies the cultural development,
Enhances the positivity around,
Beautifies the vicinity with rejoicement,
Simply saying festivals are the carriers of peace.

60. AIM FOR THE GOAL

Aim for the goal
Rightly said - But what is the goal?
It's not a fixed one.
In every step of our life, goal changes
Completion of schooling with "A" grade
Perhaps to be the goal of children,
Youths' goal goes along with their
Dream college of passion field,
Getting a job and having a settled life,
Owning a house satisfying domestic needs,
Little sophistication, then passing dreams
To our children and thus goes on our goals.
With God's grace we chase them with will power.

61. EVERY CLOUD HAS IT'S SILVER LINING

Every coin has it's other side,
Every night has it's day,
Every darkness symbolises a hidden brightness,
Every failure leads to the success.
Night prepares us for a next day by relaxing,
Darkness makes us realise the significance of brightness,
Without setbacks man couldn't step
Every cloud has it's silver lining.

62. I AM....

I am the mistress of my family
Holding lots of responsibilities,
With love and care I nurture
My wards with noble gesture,
At times I am a mediator,
Many a times I have to be a co-ordinator,
But all the times I am supposed to be a mentor.
Ready to serve with good virtues ever
I am a full time counsellor,
And a supporting ladder.

63. CHEMISTRY IN BOTANY

Chemistry - the study of substances,
Botany - the study of life of plants.
Chemistry in other words a perfect rapport,
The generator of vital energy suppliers,
Went hand in hand with nature.
Is it not a chemistry in botany
For a coconut shell to be hard,
Gets into our hands unbroken
Despite its height from the earth.
To maintain this chemistry
Mankind has to preserve plant life with charity.

64. IN MY VIEW, MONEY IS...

In my view money is an entry pass
To enjoy the rides of life,
But not all the rides you can go through.
There may be some you can't afford,
Some of them hired might be dormant,
In excess changes us restless,
If deficit leads to misery,
In short money makes many
But not all accept it frankly.

65. ART IS LONG

Art is long but how long

There is no measure to get along

It acts as a preservative lifelong.

Art is a diphthong,

A transition of one's creative to prolong.

Let the skill displayed be strong

Which vividly expresses the way so long

It's a form of an act to walk along.

66. THE BOND BETWEEN YOU AND ME IS..

The bond between you and me is
Like a pearl in the shell.
A wonderful playmate of my childhood,
A lovable companion of my teenage,
All time philosopher and a guide,
Giving hands to lift me up.
Yes - she is the second mother for me
Others call her as my sister.

67. I WAKE UP EARLY WHEN

I wake up early when
I am bounded with duties
Of much significance,
Of course a handful of daily duties.
Early to bed and early to rise is
The way to be healthy and wealthy,
But all these goes out in ease
For a change with holiday.
However I wish to wake up early
To make my body and mind
Feel friendly forever.

68. MIRROR REFLECTS MY...

Mirror not only exhibits the reflection
But also depicts a complete perfection,
Portrays the image as it is
No fabrication there is.
It's fine to be like a mirror
Exposing the vivid nature.
No matter what ever the scenario
With inner conscience undergo.

69. MY BLOOD BOILS..

My blood boils
When I see people spitting on the road,
Neither care for the nearby ones
Nor the social responsibility of cleanliness.
How dare to spit outside!
Sitting on the bus near the window seat
Never ever bothered about the passersby.
With an arrogant achievement on the face
The moment I see this nasty behaviour,
My mind pushes me to slap the fellow,
But my inner conscience warns me to ignore.
I too have to be self engrossed such times
As that's also a shame on me.

70. CHILDREN'S DAY WISHES

My dear children,
You are the blossoms
Spread the fragrance by your deeds,
Beautify the place with your smile,
Arise to get your rights,
Intensify your confidence,
Retain your self-respect,
Defend yourself from all evils,
Respect your elders
Acquire knowledge from scholars,
As you are the pillars of the nation.
Children's day wishes to all.

71. FORGETTING YOU IS LIKE...

Forgetting you is like
Plucking my heart and psyche.
I feel as if you were by my side
Every second hearing your voice inside,
I comfort myself with the duties leftover
I prepare my mind to forget you moreover
The thought of which goes on for the whole day
Realising that as an undone action in dismay
I polish to manage myself and booster up
To accomplish the task imposed on more stronger.

72. I CANNOT BE WITH SOMEONE WHO

I can't be with someone who

Manipulates things in a contemptuous manner,

Gossips over unwanted matter,

Seeks selfish accomplishments for time being,

Always keep an eye on others just like screening,

Acts as if like a well-wisher,

Exaggerates the trivial matters of no bother.

Simply to say - better to be alone than in bad company

73. LIFE IN LIFELESS

Life is not eternal
But life depends on lifeless eternals.
The structural entities of the universe
Reign with supremacy as panchabhutas,
How can we say those superiorities lifeless.
Much as can be seen and felt limitless
Without these lively primitive elements
Sure to say life becomes lifeless.

74. MEN'S DAY WISHES

Role of a woman exposed everywhere
Men's sacrifices known less
Duty bounded but seems to be carefree.
A perfect warden to his sister,
Lovable companion to his brother,
At times a social worker of neighbourhood,
A volunteer during menaces,
Not but the least of all
Ultimately his part succeeds
With the role of a father for his daughter.

75. SILENCE

Silence is a powerful weapon
Means a lot to sound upon.
Tool to tackle challenging quandary
Best remedy for potential crisis to carry.
Silence can deal and suggest a true solution
For many problems which even arguments can't do in resolution.
Whenever we encounter a conflict Between the mind and the heart,
Silently heed to your inner voice to act.
Restless life amidst tight schedule
A few minutes of posture in silent without any stumble.
The depth of silence brings out self reflection
Where we find ourselves linked to spiritual connection.

76. TELEVISION

1987 - some one or two houses
In our locality owned television.
I used to go to my family friend's house nearby
To watch oliyum - oliyum on Fridays,
After returning receive a lot of scoldings from my father
Despite waited for every Friday
Longing for a television at home every day.
Suddenly one day father voluntarily
Permitted to go there and watch.
I was so happy and eagerly went there
The hall was fully occupied with
People of all ages keenly observing,
Some old ladies crying over the scene
I sharply noted and was surprised to see
The final journey of the then CM cum great leader
All-time favourite actor - Mr. MGR.
After that incident,
We got a new television at our house shortly.

77. SECRET

Secret of life is success,
Secret of success is hardwork,
Secret of hardwork is diligence,
Secret of diligence is intention,
Secret of intention is desire,
To reap the ultimate secret
Reveal the hidden secret,
Of your unrevealed deeds.
Make sure of it's desirable worthiness
Then put on your deeds into actions,
Starting from your desire
There comes the true success.

78. INTROSPECTION - A COMPLETE SELF CONTEMPLATION

Says yes to positive attitudes

Warns if anything goes wrong

Hear what it says

Act accordingly to go strong.

Explore your mental ability,

Examine your thoughts and emotions,

Perceive them with morality,

Analyse the truth of this creation.

The Creator has sent for some purpose

It won't be fair if we simply leave.

Leave some scars of goodness on your part

At least ask your mind what have you done so far.

Sketch out the things of our ability

With this complete introspection

The objective of life becomes meaningful.

79. SPILT WORDS

Spilt words cannot be taken back
The marks left by them live long.
Think over thrice before uttering,
Once fallen regret without lag,
Make sure to evade them hereinafter.
Do hesitate for usage of inappropriate words
Take into account of soft and humble words in hands.
A gentle word is equivalent to a thousand words of wisdom
Let the spilt words be soothing words of comfort
Make the discouraging and harsh words
Vanish in our vocabulary,
Henceforth a blissful life welcomes you.

80. GOOD THINGS HAPPEN WHEN...

Good things happen when
We are prepared for any plight,
Not letting down the confidence level
To accept life as such blessed with,
Fulfil the duties with utmost satisfaction
By being good and doing good,
Sowing positive thoughts to reap
A good fortune for future
Not envying others development,
Avoid gossiping over unwanted issues,
Take the good ones surrounding leaving the bad behind
Eventually trust on the creator for the happenings.

81. MY WAY IS TOWARDS

My way is towards
Not what I had decided,
Changes according to the situation
Sometimes I may not be able to go
In a particular path of my wish.
I need to prefer the other
To satisfy the dependents
At times my way opens for me
Like our Creative Writers group,
To co-ordinate my way and desire.
We need a starter at every stage
With that hold I just made up my mind
Holding thus the journey goes on.

82. ATTENTION PLEASE

• 82 •

Your attention please, dear ego

Here is an announcement exclusively for you

Almost all the human heart's door closed for you,

Better you seek entry into an inhabited land

Where you can search of people in demand.

If at all you made an entry into the heart

Definitely you will be blocked at the spot,

Without the knowledge of your arrest

There would be a chase of no rest.

On the hunt for chase weariness accompanies

On complete exhaustion I can see the egoism perishes.

83. THE WORLD NEEDS MORE OF

Many valuable qualities

Very much dwindling nowadays.

Lack of sympathy has taken over kind,

Selfishness has penetrated into the minds of our beings,

Taking revenge has become a heroic deed,

Enjoying pleasure in others bleed,

Expropriating the wealth and wisdom of society,

Eradicate all those filthy thoughts and greed without anxiety.

Enroot the young with good virtues,

Discard all the mediocre attributes,

Nourish them the noble cause of humane,

Reap the rewards of the best mankind what the world needs more.

84. WHOLE WORLD IN OUR HANDS

Whole world in our hands
In the form of mobiles,
Whatever we need to know,
We expect - all with a say no.
In search of one many unknowns
Open for us unwittingly
A boon or a bane, we won't go for a debate
Without our knowledge we go for unnecessary display
Be sure to take it for granted,
Beware of unvalued releases,
Be like a swan to segregate,
Unnecessary and necessary.

85. ONE THING I ADMIRE IN YOU IS...

There's not a thing to admire you
Hope I can say that to pursue
So many things I admire in you
Not discrete to review.
Shall I say about your vastness
Or shall I point out the saltiness
You are the major producer of O2,
Needless to say a provider of substantial suppliers of food.
Moreover even when I see you
A whole day I will not be bored,
Rather you pacify me gently patting the feet
Ahoy! My admiral sea!!

86. CARING FOR DIFFERENTLY ABLED

Cast away the habit of pitying
In lieu make them undaunted.
Light the lamp in their lives prettying,
Help them to grow with inner strength,
Hold by not letting down their self confidence,
Mould them to travel life line at length,
With all the potentials of full persistence.
Differently abled - Abled in peculiar tasks,
Expose your skills,
Exhibit your talents,
Encourage yourselves,
Establish your powers,
Enrich your capabilities,
You need nobody to care for you.

87. ANTS - THE LESSONS I LEARNT FROM YOU

Your social behaviour,
Planning for the future,
Industriousness, well organized nature,
Untired and invigorating labour,
Eusocial colonial insect
Of superhuman strength
Highly self-disciplined in its path,
Without missing every prospect.
Your organised colonies stress
The way of living together.
You are the premier soil turner
Although not so mentions on ecological facts.
A good decision maker - What else to learn from you dainty ants.

88. THE WORST KIND OF SUFFERING IS..

Hunger - a great threat to humanity

Hunger itself is a heart rending state.

Hunger in tender is ghastly

Behind this horrible scenario is fate

Will say some apathists.

It's a matter of concern globally.

Origin of crime is where hunger starts

This environmental issue to be cared psychologically.

Poverty, the basic cause of hunger

Arising of the unequal distribution of income,

Leading to social discrimination factor

Enhanced income generating activities - a key to sustain income.

Hunger free world

Pinnacle with crowned.

89. A WISE WOMAN ONCE SAID..

The creator gives the bearings
Upto the limit to bear upon
He also conceals a hidden solution.
Only thing is to reveal and accept
The truth of the happenings.
She also stated not to blame for it
As it's the game on His part to play on.
What is given to us in the name of Karma
Should be performed by all means,
That wise woman is none
Other than my mom.
I was not conscious of these words
In days of yore.
Today I realise her sayings
Thank you my dear mom.

90. WHEN I CAN'T DECIDE WHERE TO GO

Simply leave the matter as it is,

Wait for the time to come out of that.

Some happenings make me feel

Even god has abandoned.

But in due course one can realise

Nothing happens for no cause.

Only the time that becomes

The decision maker at trying situations

Leave some span to pop out

Definitely a hopeful way opens

With a guidance to move further

Follow the light of the right path without hesitation.

91. THE REAL WEALTH IS..

Not to expect others help
For the basic needs till the end of the life.
Particularly at the end
No bed ridden survival for ever.
Slumber embraces with a Lullaby
As soon as I lay down on the bed.
Feeling safety in my comfort zone
Fulfilling the wishes of near and dears
A complete self satisfaction in my tasks.
Positive and good vibes to acknowledge,
Kind hearted people around to care,
Most supportive relatives to share ups and downs,
Oh Almighty! Bestow these real wealths on me.

92. BLOOD DONATION - A GREAT SERVICE

So many services,
So many donations,
Either for fame or name
Stood upon with bragging.
Yes, of course every service counts the most.
Blood donation has a unique place for having
Holding lives of many at the verge.
Nothing can compensate this charity
Maintain the purity of your blood
Come forward whole heartedly
To be a life saver rather than a donor.

93. DEAR SOLDIERS

The real heroes of motherland,
Not only the warriors but also the defenders
Throughout the year strive hard
For the homeland not bothering about own homes.
Sacrifices of their lives are visible
Innumerable relinquishments of their
Precious, cherishable lifetime moments,
Passing away in them are invisible
Hats off to the truthful native soil lovers.

94. MATH - GENIUS RAMANUJAN

Mathematics - Not a subject
it's a life oriented lesson.
One of the mathematical geniuses
Profound knowledge in number theory,
In-depth intellect in infinite series,
Founder of Hardy-Ramanujan number,
Self taught mathematician behind many theorems,
Presented his papers on intuitions,
Paved way to multiple discoveries,
Could have been the one to solve
Many unknown theories if lived for some more years,
The unsolved theorems left are still waiting to be proved
Feeling proud to be a maths teacher
Blessed to have studied in this legend's schooling.

95. THE BEST GIFT I WISH TO GIVE YOU IS ..

My dear children,
The valuable virtues of life
To stand by your side in all steps of your career,
A moral supporter through out the lifetime,
Providing the best education of your choices,
A supporting ladder to reach the peak,
All-time guide for a pleasant Iife,
A good role model of your inspiration,
A helping hand at times of needs,
Above all, an all round counsellor,
Of the most a good friend of you ever dears.

96. COUNT YOUR BLESSINGS

Blessed for the birth of a human,
Blessed to be a woman,
Blessed with gifted parents,
Blessed to be a teacher,
Blessed with a contented life,
Blessed to have a amicable children,
Blessed to be a being of good fortune.
Inspite of some misfortunes
As it's our duty to accept both
Yet taught a lot for the remaining part
It's time to thank the Almighty
For the countless blessings.

97. LAUGH AND THE WORLD LAUGHS WITH YOU

Share your happiness with all
See the enjoyment in them.
Some relish, some envy behind the smiles
Whatever ecstasy prevails as if
The whole surrounding rejoicing with us.
The gloomy environment is not
Such a state of the former,
Don't always think everyone will take part
In your unhappiness on real
It's wise to have no such expectations.
I always like walking in the rain
So no one can see me crying- Charlie Chaplin.

98. THE TRUE JOY IN LIFE IS...

Accept the life as such,

Be benevolent with others,

Consider the feelings of people around,

Dedicate yourself to your profession,

Establish good thoughts,

Fragrance with smile,

Garnish with good ethics,

Help to the needful,

Ignore the backbiters,

Justify the actions,

Kind enough to all,

Leave the annoying issues,

Modify your efforts according to the situation,

Never give up the mind.

99. ONCE UPON A TIME

Once upon a time,
When there were no miseries
Ecstasy was the only thing known
No commitments, no quandaries,
No problems, no pressures,
All the time wondered about
How to enjoy and share the happiness.
Restrictions of course prevailed
That too we took it for granted.
Egoism deserted, hatredness departed,
Foxiness fled, basic needs fulfilled.
Oh! Yearning for the bygone days
Which had gone out of reach.

100. NAMESTRY

M - Merciful

A - Affectionate

R - Responsible

A - Amiable

G - Good hearted

A - Assertive

T - Tender hearted

H - Heuristic

A - Adjustable

M - Maternal

About The Author

Mrs. U. Maragatham, M.Sc., M.Ed., M.Phil.,Graduate Teacher (Maths), Sri Saraswathi Patasala GHSS, Kumbakonam, Thanjavur dt.

Mrs U. Maragatham M.Sc.,M.Ed.,M.Phil., graduate in mathematics presently working in Sri Saraswathi Patasala Girls Higher Secondary School, Kumbakonam, Thanjavur district. She has nearly 17 years of teaching experience in a matric school and 5 years in aided school. She has a great passion on English language and started writing poems during the lockdown period with the help of Creative Writers Group run by Mrs. D. Brinda and supported by many eminent English teachers. She is very much interested in reading and writing. Her ultimate goal is to make her students expertise in LSRW skills. She has been practicing the students in the abovesaid and engaging them in various activities in Kalvi online radio. As the next step in her writing journey, she has planned to make her children write short stories in Tamil and English and planning to publish it as a book and the work is under process. At present she has been assigned to work on the Children's magazine by our Education Department, as the District Co-ordinator. She wants to be a good writer and awaiting to put up the best on her part in the days to come.